Contents

Making Joyful Space

Foreword by Sebastian Tombs, chief executive, Architecture and Design Scotland

Architecture matters. The more susceptible we are to our built environment, the more it matters – hence the importance of understanding the relationships between young children, places and spaces.

Architecture and Design Scotland (A+DS) is a non-departmental public body established by the Scottish Executive in April 2005 to raise awareness, stimulate ambition and encourage best practice in the built environment. A+DS supports Making Space because it sends a clear message advocating excellence and diversity – and joy – in designing for the young.

Design comprises a mix of different skills, combining the analytical and the synthetic. It goes without saying that buildings must function well, be responsive to the local climate and use materials wisely. But to achieve more – to handle movement patterns, maximise light and air and create a place that is welcoming and uplifting – this requires a creative spark. Increasing volumes of research show direct correlations between the qualities of educational spaces and learning outcomes. Designing for the young is thus a heavy responsibility, requiring a deft touch. Far from being straightforward, it is a real challenge.

An essential principle is the appropriate involvement of users. The more opportunity for user engagement with the brief, the greater the chances of effective design solutions. A building project can provide significant opportunities for learning, even with the youngest children. The examples shown here vary considerably in the ways the teams of clients, users and designers have worked together; readers will have to decide the extent to which the results match the aspirations and the processes deployed to achieve them.

There is currently much debate as to what constitutes local – or national – character and Scotland is well served by much of its built inheritance in this regard. A close reading of context (social, economic, environmental and cultural) is essential, but it is important to be able to move beyond the past to solutions appropriate for tomorrow. This is a voyage of discovery and experimentation; a sharing of different approaches and resolutions. Scotland as a nation has always had an international outlook and its current architectural energy, with public policy support, has culminated in effective European outreach, taking in – for example – the Venice Biennale.

In the words of the first minister:

> "The quality of Scotland's built environment is important, not only to our own quality of life, but to the perception of the country abroad as an outstanding place to be."

This publication is aimed at clients and policymakers, to focus attention on the need for thoughtful and context-sensitive design for the young, in accordance with the United Nations Convention on the Rights of the Child:

> "… recognising the right of the child to rest and leisure, to engage in play and recreational activities appropriate to the age of the child and to participate freely in cultural life and the arts."

United Nations Convention on the Rights of the Child, Article 31

I hope this volume succeeds in stimulating better design for the young; Architecture and Design Scotland is pleased to be able to support its publication.

Sebastian Tombs

Sebastian Tombs
chief executive
Architecture and Design Scotland

left: birds nest swing, Kleine Arche kindergarten, Germany

Introduction and overview

Bronwen Cohen, chief executive, Children in Scotland

When architects, planners, educators, psychologists, brain scientists and children are brought together to consider the design and use of space the results are worth recording. *Making space: award-winning designs for young children* is such a record. It celebrates the ideas and designs that came out of an international award and conference on architecture and design for young children, and a filmed conversation and art competition for children themselves.

These events came about when *Children in Europe*, a periodical published by a network of magazines across the European Union, decided to look at the issue of architecture and design for young children. A coalition of agencies in Scotland (Children in Scotland, the Royal Incorporation of Architects in Scotland and the Scottish Executive) and internationally (Children in Europe and the Organisation for Economic Co-operation and Development) came together to take forward some of the issues it raised.

So what are some of the issues we identified in examining architecture and design for young children?

Space to play

In many countries more young children are spending time in organised childcare of some kind and have less access to safe public space. Whilst young children have less freedom to roam, a survey by *Children in Europe* magazine, issue 8, showed that services are also offering less space. Indoor and outside space requirements for services for young children have been reduced in a number of countries and many countries have no specific requirement or recommendation about the amount of external space necessary for each child. The *Children in Europe* survey also found that concepts of safety vary widely – in the UK, for example, health and safety requirements often mean young children will not have access to activities such as carpentry or tree-climbing, which are commonplace in Nordic countries.

Finnish architect Pihla Meskanen *(p.17)* reports on the constraints of current lighting legislation as she seeks to create environments where children can create their own worlds through the use of light and shade. Elena Rocchi, a Catalan architect, describes how she has used water safely and successfully in playgrounds and parks in Barcelona *(p.14)*. Space requirements and health and safety legislation may be matters for those responsible for legislation or guidance but are also challenges for architects and designers: how to make the most of available space and how to offer children better opportunities to explore whilst managing risk.

left: cladding detail, Fawood Children's Centre, London – runner-up in the international architecture award

"Why do children seek out the untidy or incomplete, ruined buildings or building sites? Buildings that offer young children the chance for them to re-order, complete or knock down like sandcastles on the beach, provide their brains with room to grow and mature."

Matti Bergstrom and Pia Ikonen,
Children in Europe, **Issue 8**

Room to grow and learn

What kind of space do children need to enable them to meet, play and learn about themselves? Our rapidly increasing knowledge of how the brain develops is now contributing to this discussion. Finnish neurophysiologist Professor Matti Bergstrom and his colleague Pia Ikonen have pointed to the role of nature and 'empty' space in nourishing the brain's ability to learn and develop. Nature kindergartens offer children the opportunity to create their own 'possibility' or 'fantasy' world whilst built space, they say, should contain lots of empty space which children can fill themselves. Italian architect Michele Zini argues that children benefit from a stimulating environment that offers different possibilities for experimenting and investigating: a rich sensory world where children "above all, feel loved".

Anne Meade *(p.13)* describes ways in which New Zealand communities have sought to reflect the natural environment and Maori traditions.

Collaboration in design

There is widespread agreement that the planning and design of children's spaces should be a collaborative process but how best to achieve this? Bringing all the stakeholders together is a good start, but throughout the Making Space programme, the benefits of systematic collaborative processes such as the American architect, Bruce Jilk's 'design down' process *(p.22)* and English architect Mark Dudek's work *(p.22)*, became evident. Stakeholder involvement is essential in making decisions in a rapidly changing society but it also, as a process, builds and supports community links that endure beyond the construction and opening of a building.

left top: playgrounds in New Zealand use traditional Maori designs from the past – still very culturally significant for Maori in the present day.

left below: parents in New Zealand get involved in redesigning an outdoor area at a pre-school.

Andrea: Let's put a big long shelf here...

Stefano: Why don't we put the building site here...

Carlo: Yes, the building place has to be big...

Three-year-olds on their first day at the Giacosa Infant School, Milan, Italy – *Children in Europe*, Issue 8

Going down a rainbow by Jade Williamson, Balhousie Primary School, Perth – Winner of Children in Scotland's national art competition, My Favourite Place

Involving young children in design

Children are the least powerful of stakeholders and are too easily ignored. The pictures from the My Favourite Place art competition *(p.28)* and Access All Areas consultation *(see below)* show that children have some compelling messages for architects and designers. As UK researcher Alison Clark argues *(p.25)*, taking time to listen to young children and finding ways of helping them express their views can contribute to new design possibilities. Moreover, this right of children to have their opinions heard is a right that is protected by European law.

As holders of rights even the youngest children are entitled to express their views, which should be given due weight ... Young children are acutely sensitive to their surroundings and very rapidly acquire understanding of the people, places and routines in their lives.

United Nations Convention on the Rights of the Child – General comment on Article 12

Access all areas

Understanding that accessibility is about far more than physical access is one of the most prominent themes to have emerged from an ongoing consultation with school pupils in the Scottish Borders, UK, on how to improve school life for children with additional support needs. The consultation of primary and secondary school pupils revealed that for children, accessibility in its widest sense is as much about friendship and feeling included as it is about being able to access a building, and that this has particular implications for those children with learning and behavioural difficulties.

For more information visit www.childreninscotland.org.uk/html/par_acc.htm

"Never has there been a better opportunity to create high quality spaces for children, and people must grasp that opportunity. Good architecture is as important for children as it is for adults. Giving children access to high quality spaces is a part of giving them the best start in life."

UK journalist and broadcaster Kirsty Wark, chair of Making Space: architecture and design for young children conference, Edinburgh, Scotland, December 2005

Designing for involvement

Young children can contribute to the design of space. But should we not also be considering ways in which design can facilitate their involvement in services in other ways?

Norwegian architect Karin Buvik has suggested that eco-friendly buildings which make provision for children to be involved in monitoring their environmental impact can engage young as well as older children (p.30).

The architects for the award-winning Saint Therese Nursery in Reunion Island in the Indian Ocean used the bioclimatic design of the building to awaken the children to the local geography and environment (p.37).

Finnish architect Pihla Meskanen (p.17) makes the case for architecture education to enable children to understand, evaluate and contribute to their environment.

So where do we go now?

Services for young children have struggled to attract the attention of architects and designers: funding in many countries has often focused on developing places and not encouraged an aspirational approach to the design of buildings or the external space which young children use. But as Richard Yelland, head of the Programme on Public Educational Building at the OECD told the conference, this could be changed in the European Union if countries implemented the financial target, proposed over ten years ago by the European Commission's Childcare Network, of spending one per cent of their Gross Domestic Product on pre-school services.

Certainly, the quality of design in countries such as Sweden and Finland, which are spending well over this target, demonstrate this. In the UK, current school building programmes – which include pre-school services as well as schools – offer opportunities for more and better design. To date, these possibilities have been vastly under-used, reflecting, in part, the more marginalised status of pre-school services and the problems this creates for funding mechanisms. In England, the capital programme associated with the SureStart programme provided a significant boost to the building of services evident in the entries to the international award, with new SureStart centres in Tamworth, West Midlands and Pen Green, Northamptonshire.

This publication offers everyone the opportunity to see the award-winning designs and captures some of the discussion which took place at the conference itself. It is intended to encourage further discussion of what constitutes good design for services, as well as raising all of our aspirations for the spaces we offer our young children.

Scotland has seen some world-class design in services for young children, such as the Cowgate Centre in Edinburgh *(pictured left)*. It is an excellent example of an innovative use of space right in the urban heart of the city. More significant in the Scottish entries for the award has been a heartening emphasis on involving children in the design of their own space. The voices of young children themselves come through loud and clear in the design of the Darnley Park play area in Stirling *(pictured below)*.

"We're making footprints. We're doing it in sand and you put your foot in it and it makes a pattern."

"We're here to check out where to put our handprints."

"You need to choose where you put them [footprints and handprints]. The reason why I put it here is you can sit on it as a little seat and you can stand on it to see what people are doing."

Children talking about their involvment in the development of Darnley Park, Stirling, Scotland

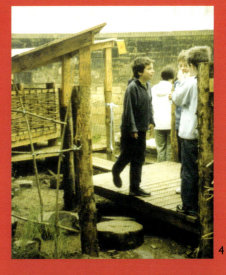

1. Cowgate Centre, Edinburgh, Scotland
3. Darnley Park, Stirling, Scotland

2. PHEW Respite Centre, Motherwell, Scotland
4. Glasgow Steiner School, Scotland

1: Space to play

"Building for young children should contain a lot of empty space with possibilities and to have free choice... Of course, we also need order and structure. But spaces that have four straight walls like the classrooms in many of our schools are not what is required."

Matti Bergstrom and Pia Ikonen, Space to play, room to grow, *Children in Europe*, Issue 8

Professor Bergstrom believes that space to play and explore worlds of 'possibility' is a vital ingredient in children's brain development.

In Norway this sense of 'space' and 'possibility' is best captured in its nature kindergartens, where children are outdoors all day. As Anders Farstad, nursery teacher at Hval Gaard nature kindergarten says: "In Norway we have a saying: 'There's no such thing as bad weather, only bad clothing'."

There is a strong tradition of being close to nature in Norway, and this also helps to develop a sense of belonging and identity. Being outdoors all the time carries significant health benefits in that children are not in enclosed in centrally heated spaces all day; instead they are outside being active and getting lots of exercise. Even in ordinary kindergartens in Norway, space is usually provided to allow infants to sleep outdoors.

This appreciation of the value of nature and the outdoors is reflected in much of the architecture in Norway. There is a very strong element of ecological design in Norway with its EcoBuild programme, which was launched in 1997.

The Kvernhuset Secondary School *(p.12)* integrates the building and playground's environmental dimension into the everyday life of the school, explains Karin Buvik. The building was designed to be environmentally friendly, capturing natural and renewable resources – sunlight, water and wind – to be used for heating, lighting and ventilation. It was also designed to make use of the existing site qualities. Materials such as wood and granite from the site were used for the build, and the layout was designed to preserve existing trees as much as possible.

Environmental aspects were taken into consideration when planning pupil journeys to and from the Kvernhuset School. The goal was to enable all pupils to reach the school by themselves, either on foot or by bicycle, and minimise the use of cars and buses. This was achieved through the construction of bicycle paths, sub passages and pedestrian crossings.

left: in nature kindergartens in Norway, children are outdoors all day, being active and getting lots of exercise

"We don't need a lot of toys outdoors. Nature has almost everything we need. The children experiment and learn how to use trees, water, floes, snow, ice, and so on. It stimulates their curiosity. We see the children learn that co-operating with others is vital if you are to succeed, especially in solving the different problems or tasks given to them during the day. We show them how to use simple tools such as knives and saws, how to light a fire, and so on."

Anders Farstad, nursery teacher at Hval Gaard nature kindergarten, Norway

Kvernhuset Secondary School in Norway was built making use of existing site materials such as wood and granite. The layout was designed so as to preserve the existing trees as much as possible.

The outdoors is captured and reflected inside the school building too. Places where trees once stood are marked by tree trunks, and indeed, some of the existing trees themselves are left intact, as are natural rock formations, helping the children learn about their local natural environment.

New Zealand is a land of forests, mountains, huge areas of green space and a large coastline. The landscape is closely integrated into everyday life, and, as in Norway, contributes significantly to a sense of culture and identity. Maori people call themselves *tangata whenua*, which translates as people of the landscape. For them, relationships with their ancestors and the places from where they originated are of utmost importance. "Place – the social and the cultural – is foregrounded," says Anne Meade, co-ordinator of the Early Years Childhood Centres of Innovation in New Zealand.

The indoor environments of early childhood centres in New Zealand are similar to those in most western countries. Sometimes, special design features, such as images from the sea or land, birds or animals, or Maori symbols, are incorporated into the design. Elements from the outside are often brought inside, such as sea shells, stones, drift wood, bark, flowers and seeds. These help provide learning opportunities for the children to study, play with or create things from. Conversely, indoor objects, such as beanbags and books, are often brought outside. This opens up possibilities in the use of available space.

It is common in New Zealand to have large areas of outdoor space, both in family homes, and early childhood centres. In fact, because the outdoors has such cultural significance for New Zealanders, access to it by children is viewed as a right, which is protected in law:

[There must be] adequate space for different types of indoor and outdoor play, including individual and group activities ... The outdoor space must be close enough to the indoor space as to allow for quick, easy, and safe access by children.

Education (Early Childhood Education) Regulations 1998, Part 3, 17 (2, 3)

This translates into spaces that allow indoor-outdoor flow as much as possible throughout the day. Research by Alison Stephenson at the Victoria University of Wellington found that children actively choose to spend more than half of their time outside (*Opening up the outdoors: A reappraisal of young children's outdoor experience,* a Med. Thesis 1998).

The outdoors has strong cultural significance for New Zealanders, and children's right to access outdoor space is protected in law.

Plaza at the Museu d'Art Contemporani de Barcelona, Spain

"Outdoors, children take more risks and call 'Look at me'; indoors, children request: 'Look at what I've made'.

Outdoors, children and adults are constantly changing equipment and materials; indoors the layout is fairly permanent.

Outdoors, freedom is prevalent; indoors there is more control of behaviour.

Outdoors, teachers move in and out of interactions and give skill instructions; indoors, teachers can be ambivalent about joining in.

Outdoors is seen as an open environment that has more potential for children's theorising."

'Place and space', Anne Meade,
Children in Scotland, Dec 2005

Outside space offers several valuable features. Outdoor playing areas can consist of sand, dirt and water, all of which appeal to the senses. Gardening, making compost and growing vegetables and herbs provide learning opportunities. The outdoors is a changing environment, in terms of nature, seasons, times of day and weather, and so it encourages children to adapt and learn from the changing conditions. The outdoors also provides more space to move around in, to explore, retreat, create, be physically active. It can also encourage social interaction – children playing together, adults engaging with children, and parents joining in too.

Darnley Park is an example of an outdoor play space in Scotland, and is one of the winning designs of the architecture competition *(p.40)*. With its rope bridge, hills to allow for climbing and sledging, and space left wild to explore, it successfully manages to combine a space that allows freedom to play imaginatively, with health and safety legislation. As Sue Gutteridge, play services manager at Stirling Council Children's Services, says: "It challenges the limitations often imposed on children's play through misplaced health and safety concerns."

Enric Miralles Benedetta Tagliabue EMBT Arquitectes Associats, based in Barcelona, has created many challenging outdoor environments in Spain, Germany, Japan and the Netherlands.

As architects Elena Rocchi and Benedetta Tagliabue explain, the use of water in Diagonal Mar Park was critical because the park was directly connected to the sea. There are health and safety regulations to be navigated but mostly it is just a common sense approach that is needed to achieve the balance between creating stimulating and challenging spaces which are also safe for children to play in. As Rocchi and Tagliabue explain: "The more the place is 'dangerous', the more you watch out. It is the natural instinct of survival."

"I like going off on nature walks when there's lots of things to explore, especially in the woods."

Child from Sathya Sai School, St Andrews, Scotland – Children's Voices film

left: Kleine Arche kindergarten, Huenxe, Germany
above: Ikiminami primary school, Japan

"The playground, at the end, is always something that, as much as you plan, you will never guess totally. Imagination has no rules."

Elena Rocchi and Benedetta Tagliabue, EMBT architects, Barcelona, Spain

above left and centre: Diagonal Mar Park, Barcelona, Spain,
above right: on top of the roof at Santa Catarina market, Barcelona, Spain

2: Room to grow and learn

"Architecture education aims to develop a child's ability to perceive, consider, understand, conceptualise and evaluate his or her environment. It supports the development of individual cultural identity, which connects us to our local surroundings, to our country and to humankind.

Pihla Meskanen, architect and founder member of Arkki School of Architecture, Finland

Buildings, such as schools, nurseries, and kindergartens, are places where children are encouraged to learn and explore. However, the design process itself and any well-designed building for children can provide opportunities for learning.

In Finland, it is the right of every citizen to be taught about their built and natural environment, so they can share in the responsibility for it – something the Finnish government views as being a vital part of citizenship. This is the main objective of the Arkki School of Architecture for Children and Youth. Arkki provides tools to help children understand, evaluate and critically analyse their surroundings, and to help them understand the impact of the built environment on the welfare of individuals and society as a whole.

At Arkki, they experiment with 'possibility worlds' by allowing children the opportunity to create spaces in 1:1 scale using materials that have been carefully selected and designed to be lightweight and easy to move. Experimenting with different types of materials – translucent, transparent and opaque – and different forms of lighting, creates infinite possibilities. Says Meskanen: "Creating 'possibility worlds' promotes the understanding of basic elements in architecture. At the same time it emphasises the joy of learning and discovering."

Lighting is very important in creating flexible spaces. However this comes into conflict with legislation in Finland, as in many countries, where the legislation sets out certain minimum requirements for lighting. As Meskanen comments, these minimum requirements become the standard and the only way to create lighting within buildings.

"The minimum becomes the maximum, and there is no alternative. In typical school building projects flexible lighting is not yet understood as a means to create versatile learning environments."

Pihla Meskanen

left: the Indian Teepee – children learn about cultural context, history and traditions at the Arkki School of Architecture, Finland

Pupils' recommendations for new toilets included placing mirrors away from sinks to avoid hair blocking drains and queues for sinks.

The process of design can provide learning opportunities for children. Scotland's The Lighthouse project, Design for Learning: Schools for the 21st Century, showed how involving children in the design process is a learning opportunity for the children themselves, helping to develop skills, responsibilities and experiences which they would not have developed through school education alone.

"Through the projects, pupils developed not only their aspirations for future learning and teaching and for design but also critically engaged in exploring the values and assumptions behind the design process and the resultant designs."

Anne Cunningham, project co-ordinator, Design for Learning: Schools for the 21st Century project, Scotland

One of the key successes of the project was in developing strategies for supporting adults and professionals to be learners and to learn from children and young people.

In the nature kindergartens of Norway, nature provides a wealth of learning experiences. Where better to learn about trees, plants and animals that to be amongst them, observing, exploring and interacting with them?

Michele Zini, Italian architect and designer of Tetra Pak nursery (p.38), one of the winning entries of the international architecture award, also believes the environment can have a profound impact on children's development. Spaces for children provide an important interface between children and the world they live in, allowing them to interact with other children, adults, animals, plants and objects.

"When we are born, our brain and our capacity to perceive and experience reality are not yet formed and defined, but like a flower bud, are waiting to open. We develop our senses and cognitive abilities through interaction with our environment."

Michele Zini, architect of Tetra Pak nursery and researcher with Reggio Children and Domus Academy Research Centre, Italy

"Light and shade are some of the most important components in architecture. Usually the most poetic or most impressive spaces are created by moulding the space with light and shadow. Various kinds of atmospheres can be created by using different ways of directing the natural light in the space."

Pihla Meskanen, architect and founder member of Arkki School of Architecture, Finland

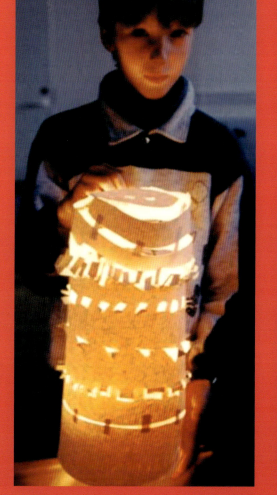

above: various studies of light and shadow at Arkki School of Architecture, Finland

Although children's brains continue to develop until the end of adolescence, it is in the early years that the development is most formative. Young children are constantly absorbing and processing information and sensations from the world around them. In this way, says Zini: "Children are a laboratory for the senses with each sense activating other senses. They have a synaesthesic capacity: they 'see' temperature, they 'touch' light, they 'taste' smells." Buildings and spaces for young children can, in this way, be viewed as being "an enormous workshop of the senses".

Thus, believes Zini, good design for children should provide a "rich stimulating environment that offers many different possibilities for experimenting, investigating, verifying and developing". It should create an environment "where children can see, touch, hear, taste, smell, play, explore and experiment and, above all, feel loved."

Developing flexible, generic spaces that can be adapted to different purposes at different times of the day helps to maximise the possibilities. This generic space can be viewed as a piazza or town square, a central area children are free to use as they wish – to play, read or watch others – leaving other areas to be more specialised and fulfil specific functions such as the kitchens or areas that require a lot of technology, such as music rooms or classrooms.

Karin Buvik also believes that good design for children should include flexible spaces. She refers to a "bazaar" model where there is a central thoroughfare which is also a point of meeting and mixing, and from which, rooms – where doors can either be open or closed depending on their use – extend.

Design which stimulates the senses makes use of colour, light, sound, smell and texture. Colour can be used to create subtle shades, contrasts and variety which produce a rich visually stimulating environment and to delineate specific spaces, areas or objects. Lighting can be varied, coming from a range of different sources, including natural light – children frequently complain of the lack of this in school buildings – and making use of shadow as well as light. Enabling the intensity of lighting to be modified by staff and children also allows them to use spaces flexibly.

The materials used in the building should also be rich and varied, creating, what Zini calls "a multi-sensory setting with surfaces that are smooth and rough, wet and dry, opaque, bright, translucent, and transparent". There should be some features which change over time, such as wood, stone, flowers and fabrics, and some features that remain unchanged, such as glass and steel.

Furniture has a part to play and should be interesting and stimulating, as well as being safe and of suitable dimensions, to fulfil their purpose. Lightweight, moveable furniture helps to maximise flexibility.

Sound is an equally important consideration. Some areas are naturally noisy and other areas require quiet. This should be considered in the planning of a building, with sound insulation provided for rooms which are used for specifically noisy purposes such as music. Areas for quiet activities, such as reading or sleeping should be apart from the open, busy, noisy areas. For large, communal spaces, the acoustics should be given careful consideration to soften the noise as much as possible.

1. **Tetra Pak nursery, Modena, Italy** – cloakroom outside classroom (furniture: PLAY+)

2. **RAS nursery, Milan, Italy** – rest area with view to central piazza (furniture: ATELIER³)

3. **Tetra Pak nursery, Modena, Italy** – resting area for children under two (furniture: PLAY+)

4. **Nursery and pre-school, Saint Felice, Modena, Italy** – classroom and resting area on the mezzanine (furniture: ATELIER³)

photos: Antonio Marconi (number 1-3)
Miro Zagnoli (number 4)

3: Collaboration in design

"The participatory design process differs from the traditional one because the initial ideas and issues are generated by the school community which is defined broadly to include children, parents, support staff, local community groups and other interested parties, as well as teaching staff."

Rebecca Hodgson and Graham Leicester in *Designing schools for the future – a practical guide*

The traditional approach to designing spaces for children has typically been to ask one or two key people, such as the headteacher of a school, for their reactions to a design that has already been created.

Real consultation involves a wider range of stakeholders than this, including children themselves, and active encouragement of participation in the design process from the very outset.

Such a process helps identify problems and provide solutions from within the user group itself, and should lead to the creation of a building which responds to the needs of its various user groups, as well as helping to foster feelings of identity, ownership and inclusion.

Ingunnerskoli School in Iceland is a good example of the collaborative process of design. The multi-stakeholder design committee, which consisted of 40 people, including teaching and support staff, administrators, parents, architects, members of the school board and local businesses, used a design-down formula developed by US architect, Bruce A Jilk. *(Visit www.childreninscotland.org.uk/makingspace for links to the design-down formula.)*

Many of the entrants and winning designs of the international award for architecture and design for young children 2005, demonstrated good consultation of and participation by children and their communities; winners Darnley Park and Fawood Children's Centre were two such examples.

The community can play a vital part in the design, construction and funding of a building. Mark Dudek, architect on the Discovering Kids Playgroup in County Derry, Ireland, describes how the community rallied together to provide manpower and negotiate rates with local contractors to help deliver the project under its £32,000 budget.

Ingunnerskoli School, Iceland

Discovering Kids Playgroup, Ireland

Borgen Community Centre, Norway

Pen Green Centre, Corby, England

"Good consultation develops ownership and positive attitudes in users and stakeholders for the current, and future, projects. Conversely, poor consultation can undermine a project by misinforming a design brief and can result in users being disillusioned before they enter a building."

Anne Cunningham, project co-ordinator, Design for Learning: Schools for the 21st Century project, Scotland

"It [Fawood Children's Centre] is also available for training sessions, local meetings and is becoming a central hub for services for children under the age of five and their families in the area. Successful partnership between the architect, client, local education authority and headteacher has been key. The community has taken Fawood Children's Centre to its heart."

Alan Lai, architect, Fawood Children's Centre, London, England

The finished building should not be the end of the design process. As Anne Cunningham, project co-ordinator, Design for Learning: Schools for the 21st Century project, Scotland says: "This process continues once the product is in the hands of the user – a school's design is developed hourly, daily, annually, through the desire of its users."

Similarly, the collaborative process of involving communities should continue.

The Borgen Community Centre in Norway, with its secondary school, kindergarten, church, healthcare centre, youth club and outdoor facilities all on one campus, is a hub for the whole community. Not only does it provide integrated public services for the children and young people, but it has also become a centre for everyone living in the area, regardless of age, social, economical or cultural background.

The Pen Green Centre for under fives in Corby, England, can also be viewed as a hub for the community. It is a nursery school, but parents who need extra support can learn basic skills and obtain qualifications.

4: Involving children in design

"Young children are the least powerful of those involved in the building, redesigning or finishing of early childhood spaces. Their views and experiences often remain hidden from adults, who have the power to bring about change. The challenge is how to make young children's perspectives more 'visible'."

Alison Clark of the Thomas Coram Research Unit, University of London

The art competition, My Favourite Place, which was held in conjuction with the Making Space conference, showed that children have some important things to say about their spaces.

A huge range of spaces were chosen by the children, including places abroad where the family holidays, places closer to home, like the local park or a favourite walk, and places where they can indulge their hobbies, be it swimming, horseriding, dancing or playing or watching football. Bedrooms came out top as children's favourite place and it was the freedom, privacy and security of this space that children valued. The outdoors was another popular choice with the space, freedom and opportunity for play being highlighted as positive features. *(See pages 28 and 29 for the winners and quotes from some of the children who took part.)*

Alison Clark, a researcher at the Thomas Corum Research Unit, University of London, conducted research with three and four-year-olds to show how children's opinions regarding their spaces can be captured and incorporated into the design process. Using a framework known as the mosaic approach, the research involved the children taking photos of their space and the things they considered important, and also taking the adults on a guided tour through their world. This allowed a picture of the space and environment to be built up from the child's perspective.

Architects participating in the research found this process of listening to the children's ideas a very powerful one.

"It has allowed the architects to work with the children to understand not only what they 'want', but, perhaps more importantly, the thought processes behind these ideas. This becomes the 'window' into the child's way of seeing. This process has allowed the architects to move beyond the preconceptions of children's design to a new level of thinking about and designing for children."

Jennifer Singer, architect and participant in Clark's research

left: 'I love swimming' – runner-up in the 5 to 8 age category of My Favourite Place, Children in Scotland's national art competition

photo: Alison Clark

"There are many voices to be listened to in any design project. Opening up discussions may mean that differences between adults' and children's viewpoints become visible, but this can lead to new ideas."

Alison Clark, Thomas Coram Research Unit, University of London

photo: Alison Clark

above and right: children in a reception class get involved in map-making

"The sun comes through and the light goes to blue."

"If we didn't have a good team then this tent wouldn't be here."

Children from Rosewell Primary School, Scotland commenting on their outdoor shelter (pictured left)

"The sitooterie is a peaceful place. We can chat and be safe from the weather. We can play board games and we can read as well. We play there every day."

Primary seven pupils commenting on the Sitooterie (pictured right) **at Saline Primary School, Fife, Scotland**

Design for Learning: Schools for the 21st Century was a project run by The Lighthouse and funded by the Scottish Executive, which examined how to involve children in the process of designing schools. As with Clark's research, the children who participated in the design projects, were encouraged to use a wide variety of media to reveal and record their explorations, and these were incorporated into the resulting designs (p.18).

At the Arkki School of Architecture for Children and Youth children took part in a project to design a new headquarters for Save the Children in Helsinki. The children's drawings were turned into tiles, flooring and murals for decoration throughout the building.

The outdoor shelter at Rosewell Primary School in Midlothian, Scotland (entered for the architecture award and featured in the film, Children's Voices) was a good example of participatory design. As part of this project, children came up with the idea that they wanted to build something in their playground. They then drew up some ideas, which were turned into designs with the help of artist, Steve Dale. The whole school voted to decide on the winning design and parents helped raise funds to build the shelter. It is the children themselves who, through teamwork, erect the tent and help to keep it clean and tidy.

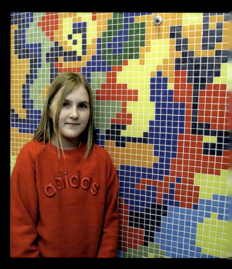

The Sitooterie was another example of the children getting involved in the design of the building. In this case a derelict building at Saline Primary School was turned into a quiet space which could also provide shelter at playtimes.

"If I had a school I'd probably have quite a lot of art in it."

"Maybe you should have a school in a tree like a big tree house."

"I like to look after the environment and that is exactly what this school does."

Children from Sathya Sai School, St Andrews, Scotland
– Children's Voices film

Designs by children at the Arkki school of architecture were turned into tiles, flooring and murals for decoration throughout the new headquarters for Save the Children in Helsinki by architects Hannu Jaakkola.

"If we do not make the effort to see things through their eyes, we could miss a multitude of opportunities to create better learning spaces for enjoyment and growth."

Robin Harper, MSP, chair of the Scottish Parliament's cross party group on children and architecture, convenor of the cross party group on children and young people, convenor of the cross party group on architecture and the built environment, co-convener of the Scottish Green Party, and judge of the art competition

UNDER 5 WINNER
Logan Bryson, Levenhall Nursery
IN THE PARK ON MY SKATEBOARD

UNDER 5 RUNNER UP
Drew Ritchie, Quarter Primary School
ON MY UNCLE JOSIE'S BIG YELLOW TRACTOR

5-8 WINNER
Eva Guidi, St Kenneth's Primary
ITALY

THE SWIMMING BATHS, I LOVE SWIMMING

5-8 RUNNER UP
Chloe Butler, Arden Primary School

OVERALL WINNER
Jade Williamson,
Balhousie Primary School

GOING DOWN A RAINBOW

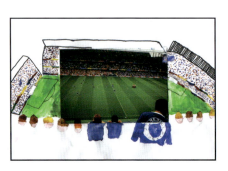

9-11 WINNER
Dominic Silk, Mile End School
STANFORD BRIDGE, CHELSEA FOOTBALL CLUB'S GROUND

9-11 RUNNER UP
Natalia Donnelly-Kay, Holy Family Primary School
MY ROOM

MY FAVOURITE PLACE!

Children in Scotland national art competition

BEST
PAINTING

MY
FAVOURITE
PLACE

Fiona Donnan, Dean Park Primary School

BEST
PHOTO

YAHOO,
I LOVE
LEAVES

Duncan Darren, Tullynessle Primary School

BEST
COLLAGE

A BEACH
IN CRETE

Catriona Salnini, Broxburn Family Centre

My favourite place is my room. I like it because I can get away from my two brothers. I have a radio in my room I got it for my birthday.

My favourite place is the television room. Because it makes me feel safe and I have a Playstation 2. I also can bring toys downstairs to play with.

My favourite place is the Meldon Hills because it's really fun to go for a picnic.

My favourite place is at the cinema because the screen is enormous and all the movies I watch are new. You have lots of popcorn, sweets and fizzy drinks.

My favourite place is the Loanhead After School club because they do fun things. It's great, more fun than bouncy castles.

My special place is my Gran's bed because she has a hot blanket and I get peace and quiet.

My special place is the library because it is quiet and has nice books. Most important I love reading them and they are free.

When I go fishing it's great. You never know when you're going to get a bite. It's quiet and relaxing. There are no cars and fumes, just lots of fresh air.

My favourite place is under my bed because at the back there's lots of space to read and because it's dark. It makes me feel safe and it 's nice and quiet and I play on my dad's laptop in there.

My favourite place is Gargunnock Hill. I like this place it's good for climbing. I go there occasionally and feel free.

5: Designing for involvement

"Why not consider future school buildings as giant laboratories? School buildings and their architecture could promote experiments in scales, shapes, colours and materials, light and shadow, natural and artificial lighting, solar power, different energy resources, energy consumption, physics, mathematics ... the list is endless."

Pihla Meskanen, architect and founder member of Arkki School of Architecture, Finland

As we have seen in chapter four, children can contribute to the design of space, but well-designed buildings can also involve children in other ways.

There are huge benefits to be derived from thinking of school buildings themselves as tools for teaching. In this way, learning becomes more than what is on the curriculum and schools become centres for learning, maximising these opportunities.

At the Kvernhuset Secondary School in south east Norway *(p.12)*, the building utilises natural and renewable energy resources, and is designed to allow the children themselves to monitor and learn about energy efficiency. In addition, part of the floor has been made from local stones, placed in order of their excavation, and artefacts of fish and animals are built into the flooring. These details attract attention and help the pupils learn about the geology and natural history of their country. "The school has proved an effective teaching tool", explains Norwegian architect Karin Buvik.

At one of the runners-up in the architecture award, Saint Therese Nursery in Reunion Island *(p.36)*, the building itself is viewed as an integral part of the children's education. The architect Philippe Zourgane describes this: "The complex geometry of the interior building space is used to awaken the children to the local geography. Because the urban settlement is growing so quickly this is vital."

Many of the entrants in the architecture award featured interactive areas to help children engage with the building; museums, in particular, provide many opportunities for this.

Sometimes this takes the form of a less formal engagement. In Plaza Angel D'Esteña, Barcelona, Spain, the surrounding walls were left blank for children to decorate. The civic centre, whose building is in the plaza, organise a new painting every month. By providing designated areas for visual expression, the temptation to grafitti elsewhere in the plaza was diminished.

Buildings and spaces which engage children not only provide learning opportunities, but also create a sense of ownership amongst the children, that the space they are using is theirs and that they are important consumers of it.

1. Museum for Children, Graz, Austria

2. Touch, Childcare Support Centre, Tokyo, Japan

3. HK Playground, Hong Kong

4. Children decorating the walls of Plaza Angel D'Esteña, Barcelona, Spain

5. Dupage Children's Museum, Chicago, USA

6. Daubeney School, London, England

7. Satuvakka Daycare Centre, Sotkamo, Finland

International School, London, England

Childcare Centre, Tokyo, Japan

Recreation park, Eskisehir, Turkey

North Point Centre, Hong Kong

Daycare Centre, Antwerp, Belgium

Nursery, Munich, Germany

Rooftop playground, New York, USA

Cowgate Nursery, Edinburgh, Scotland

Soruga Kindergarten, Japan

Primary School, de Pinte, B

Daycare centre, Sotkamo, Finland

Kindergarten, Surathani, Th

Sanitary facility, Magdeburg, Ge

'Sitooterie', Saline, Scotland

Centre for children with cancer, Jerusalem, Israel

Children's Museum, Berlin, Germany

Nursery, Utrecht, The Netherlands

Special School, Helsinki, Finland

'Continuous Children's Space', San Angel, Mexico

Daycare centre, Venice,

Daycare Centre, Kuopio, Finland

Aboriginal School, Picton, Australia

Primary School, Gujarat, India

Children's Museum, Zacatecas, Mexico

Primary School, Fukuoka, Japan

The architecture for young children international award 2005 attracted entries from as far apart as India, Turkey, USA, Colombia, England, Thailand, Scotland, France, Germany, Italy, Austria, Finland, Hungary, Japan, Hong Kong, Mexico, Israel and The Netherlands.

above: a small selection of entries to the international award 2005. All the entries can be viewed at www.childreninscotland.org.uk/makingspace

6: Making space: architecture and design for young children, international award 2005

"Working on education buildings offers a wonderful challenge and a heavy responsibility. Knowing that one's work will influence the young and their attitude to the built environment – perhaps for a lifetime."

Professor Gordon Murray, former president of the Royal Incorporation of Architects in Scotland

Over 60 entries from 17 countries all around the world were received for the architecture and design for young children, international award 2005. The winning entries were selected by a panel of judges led by Barbara Kelly OBE, and the award was presented at the Making Space conference in December 2005.

The judges were impressed with the huge range and diversity of spaces submitted, as well as the wide geographical reach of the entries, and the overall high standards of design and innovation.

Barbara Kelly said: "We were pleased to receive a huge variety of entries, from large-scale museums and schools to a small outdoor shelter or toilet block for a summer camp. Creativity, community involvement and a commitment to create the very best environments for young children possible were evident throughout. Entries came in from as far apart as New York, Delhi, Osaka and Jerusalem. Such worldwide interest is really encouraging."

The judges were looking for good designs for children: ones that appealed to the senses, that acknowledged the natural world, that encouraged participation in the designing process, that included the child's wider community into the building or space, that paid close attention to the details that matter to children, for example coats storage and toilets, and that allowed for an integrative approach to children's services.

The winning designs were selected for demonstrating these criteria.

The architecture and design for young children, international award 2005 was run by Children in Scotland and the Royal Incorporation of Architects in Scotland, in association with the Organisation for Economic Co-operation and Development and Children in Europe, with sponsorship from Lend Lease and support from the Scottish Executive.

Winner

Bubbletecture Maihara Kindergarten, Shiga, Japan

Architect firm: Shuhei Endo Architect Institute

Client: Mayor of Miahara-cho

The most striking feature of Bubbletecture, the winning entry, is its overall structure. Its continuous wave structure, made almost exclusively from natural timber, is vastly different from the four walls that normally divide up children's spaces. This has the effect of offering up a large, open, flexible space that can be used in a variety of ways, and that is not constrained by function.

The architect, Shuhei Endo, explained that this was one of the objectives of the project: "spaces for children are not able to be limited by a planner, instead these spaces should be visualized by children with their imaginations. The space for children is covered with one continuous roof. This opened space allows children to play freely … We expect that this ambiguity of space stimulates children's imaginations." This strongly echoes Professor Matti Bergstrom's belief that spaces which permit this kind of wild and creative play for children allow children's brains space to grow and mature.

The use of natural wood throughout the building, including floors, tables and chairs, is important for the architect, as wood is a traditional material in Japan, and is also safe and pleasing to the touch for the children.

Endo reports that the children enjoy the space, "running around giving a joyful voice under the big wooden structure"; they have commented on the "pleasant spaces with a lot of trees" "the shape of the roof is interesting'" and "there are varieties of the space".

The judges liked the flexibility of the space and the fact that it has a "very understandable structure, with a good balance of space that incorporates common and private space", as well as providing "a good sense of scale for small people".

1. **Different spaces retained by connection of the roof and the ground**
2. **Space under the eaves**
3. **View of playroom from corridor**
4. **Library**
5. **Playroom**
6. **Looking at the eaves from playroom**
7. **Plan**
8. **Steel joint for wooden truss**
9. **Required sizes of individual spaces define the form**

1. Sunbreakers on the exposed facades.
2. Exterior shelted atrium
3. Inside living children spaces
4. Large openings on the landscape
5. Main facade
6. Outside and inside spaces are closely mixed
7. Street level plan
8. Upper level plan
9. Cross section

1st Runner-up

Saint Therese Nusery, Reunion Island, Indian Ocean

Architect firm: RozO architecture landscape environment

Client: Mairie de La Possession

The two challenges to the architects of this nursery built on tropical Reunion Island, were the site – "slope is a geographic constant" on the island, and how to control the internal climate of the building without artificial air conditioning.

For the first challenge, the architects decided to maintain and work with the ground's natural curves and slope, and so the site was not levelled off. As the architect, Philippe Zourgane, explained: "Here, the ground is not considered as an abstract plan, as a white sheet but on the contrary, as a substance that is distorted, and optimised. The slope, the existing vegetation, the habits of the inhabitants of the district, the views hold already a potential project." Similarly, they also retained and incorporated into the design, an old wall remaining from a 19th century sugar cane factory.

For the second challenge, a bioclimatic air conditioning system was created by structuring and positioning the building to allow day and night breezes to blow right through the interior, as well as introducing shaded areas to protect from the sun.

The building's relationship with the surrounding natural environment was a key influence in its design. Zourgane said: "This nursery makes reference to the Creole way of living, in particular in its intimate outside/inside relation … The garden, the outside spaces are living spaces in themselves. The façade of the building is thought like a teared, cut out, very porous skin … there is vegetation inside and closed rooms open directly onto sheltered outside spaces. The sea and the mountain are also always visible, crossing the building in its different levels."

The simple and creative response to the site, the connection between the indoors and outdoors and sensible solution to climate control were all praised by the judges.

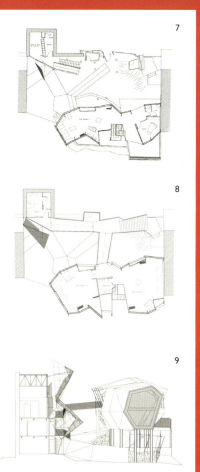

7

8

9

photographs: Antonio Marconi
furniture: PLAY+

Runner-up

Nido Stella, Tetra Pak company nursery, Modena, Italy

Architect firm: ZPZ Partners ■ Client: Tetra Pak Carton Ambient SpA

1. View to the central piazza
2. Porch at the back, facing east
3. Central piazza
4. Drawings for the prefab wooden structure

The three main considerations when designing this nursery were: to create a multi-sensorial environment, to complete it within four months, and to be ecologically sound.

The architect, Michele Zini, said: "This new building aimed to be innovative in its pedagogical approach and design. It is a multi-sensorial environment, made up of different light, colour, and materials with different surfaces and densities to encourage children to explore and develop a wide range of skills."

The nursery was completed within four months, from permission to opening. The quick construction of the nursery was due to the fact that a number of walls and the roof were prefabricated, built in Slovenia using natural wood, and then shipped over to Italy.

The nursery has been built using ecologically certified materials, including a natural wooden structure, and incorporates renewable energy resources, including solar panels, and a porch which provides shade and connects the inside to the outside.

The internal space incorporates a workshop, nap areas, soft places, spaces were children can build, a dining area, and a central public open space, known as a piazza, which can be used for many different communal purposes.

The judges particularly liked the interior design, especially "the use of transparency and varied colours. It demonstrates a clear understanding of the need to appeal to all the senses. It has good common spaces and a good effect from the porch, a space shaded and open at the same time. It also has a good ecological dimension."

Runner-up

Fawood Children's Centre, London, England

Architect firm: Alsop Design Ltd

Client: Stonebridge Housing Action Trust

Fawood Children's Centre is situated in a low-income housing estate that had a very poor image outwith the community. The centre was part of a major regenerative programme for the area.

The centre was designed through a lengthy collaborative consultation process with architects, residents, parents, children and nursery staff, all with their own different wants and needs.

As architect Alan Lai said: "Parents communicated their concerns over safety, and residents wanted to retain their pride in the centre as a community resource. The children mainly wanted trees and a lot of sand."

Once the design was agreed and approved, the building was completed within just ten months. Fawood boasts more outside learning space than inside; there are trees and space to grow flowers and vegetables, as well as the largest and deepest sandpit in the district. It also has a purpose-built stage and a Mongolian-style tent provides space for reading and computer work.

Children and their parents like the new building: "It's very child-friendly and the security is great", "It's like a theme park and gives the children plenty of opportunity to get lots of exercise", "The children are out in the fresh air without actually being outside".

The judges said: "This building is bold and dazzling but simple. It has good lighting. The design and building process involved lots of collaboration, excellent consultation and participation with the community. Indoor and outdoor space has been used very well."

The Fawood Children's Centre was also shortlisted for the Stirling prize for architecture in 2005.

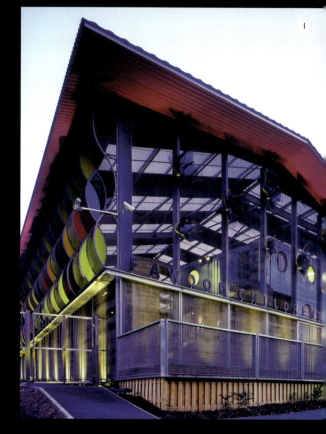

1. **South east elevation**
2. **Cycle track**
3. **Mogolion yurt**
4. **Section plan**

1. **Boardwalk promenade**

2. **Rope-net bridge (18m span) provided by Huck**

3. **3m climbing tree in centre of the park**

4. **Original concept of park design in the shape of a fish**

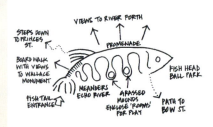

Runner-up

Darnley Park, Stirling, Scotland

Architect firm: Page & Park Architects

Play space designer: Judi Legg

Client: Stirling Council

Darnley Park play area was designed for Stirling Council to provide children and young people in the area with "a space that stimulated imaginative, non prescriptive, child-directed play in a setting that incorporated risk and challenge".

Sue Gutteridge, play services manager at Stirling Council Children's Services, said: "Children's play spaces are often nothing more than a collection of equipment on a rubber safety surface. Darnley Park, a formerly neglected city centre space, has become an enticing and, in this area of high density housing, a much needed 'play landscape'. It challenges the limitations often imposed on children's play through misplaced health and safety concerns."

The space offers loose materials including sand and grit, which can be played with and moved around. High mounds joined by a long swinging rope bridge utlilise different heights and delineate spaces, as well as provide opportunities for climbing, rolling, sliding and sledging. With the help of the children a three-metre high 'tree' built from several felled beeches has been built. The park also includes custom-built specially chosen play equipment, such as a large basket swing that can hold up to ten people at a time. Paths and decking of various textures and materials accommodate bikes, scooters and prams. Areas of space have deliberately been left wild, for the children to explore and use as they will.

The overall design of the space in the shape of a salmon was inspired by the site's views of the River Forth. A ball court forms the salmon's head, the fan tail is an attractive entrance to the park, and the fin forms the ribs that connect the park to the long flight of steps that lead from the lower part of the city up to the park, thus also increasing use of the park as a throughway.

The judges particularly liked the good consultation and participation process involving the whole community in creating the park: "the ongoing involvement of the community is very positive, an extremely successful process." They also appreciated the "clear sense of purpose to stimulate imaginative play", something that is often under-valued in design for children.

1. Classroom corridor
2. Swiming pool
3. Classroom

Runner-up

Colegio Bureche, Santa Marta, Colombia

Architect firm: Mauricio Gaviria Restrepo, Juan Manuel Peláez Freidel

Client: Associación de Amigos de Bureche

Architects of Colegio Bureche, a private bilingual school for Colombian children, were asked to design a building to reflect the school's ethos.

Juan Manuel Peláez Freidel, architect, said: "The school is committed to developing a sense of independence, joy for learning, leadership skills and a commitment to searching for a better quality of life in its pupils. The architecture is therefore not introverted or monotonously enclosing, but a space full of exciting tropical exuberance for pupils to explore and discover."

The building is surrounded by the majestic snow-capped Sierra Nevada mountains and nearby Tayrona National Park. Its linear layout, with a succession of classrooms and other areas, including a swimming pool, was chosen after careful consideration of the direction of the sun and wind. It also took into account 17 trees growing on the site, which have been left in place to provide areas of shade for pupils.

Indigenous stone and wood materials were used for the construction, as well as employing Caribbean colours for the decoration.

Pupils comments include: "The classrooms are big and have natural light" and "My school has many palm trees, a swimming pool and teachers from different cities. It is the most beautiful school in Santa Marta."

Judges commented: "This is very simple and minimalist. We liked the way it plays with different materials. It's very good for stimulating children's five senses, and has a good sense of outdoor space."

7. Summing up

**Teacher from Sathya Sai School, St Andrews, Scotland
– Children's Voices film**

There are many different spaces for children: from those designed specifically for their learning such as schools, nurseries, kindergartens; to those designed for their play, such as parks and outside spaces; and those designed to encourage their knowledge and exploration, such as children's museums and libraries; and even seemingly insignificant small spaces, such as huts, shelters, quiet rooms or outside toilets. Many were entries into the Making Space international award for architecture and design for young children. However, it should be remembered that all public space is potentially used by children, whether it is designed specifically for them or not. It is important to recognise this in the design and creation of all public space. If this is done then the result will be to make spaces that children want to use.

left: Lungomare bench, Diagonal Mar Park, Barcelona, Spain

photo: Alex Gaultier

References and resources

Children in Scotland magazine, September 2005

'International award-winners share visions of freedom'

to order: www.childreninscotland.org.uk/cis51

Children in Scotland magazine, December 2005

'Designs on my learning' by Anne Cunningham ● 'Commitment in the community' by Mark Dudek
'Place and space' by Anne Meade ● 'Worlds of possibility' by Pihla Meskanen

to order: www.childreninscotland.org.uk/cis54

Children in Europe magazine, issue 8, April 2005

'Whose space is it anyway?' by Bronwen Cohen ● 'Space to play, room to grow' by Matti Bergstrom and Pia Ikonen
'Nature: the space provider' by Anders Farstad ● 'See, hear, touch, taste, smell and love' by Michele Zini
'Bringing the outside inside' by Karin Buvik ● 'Design down: collaboration for long-term investment' by Bruce A Jilk
'Time to listen: young children's perspectives on design' by Alison Clark

to order: www.childreninscotland.org.uk/html/cie8

Children, spaces, relations: metaproject for an environment for young children
edited by Michele Zini and Giulio Ceppi (Domus Academy, Reggio Children 1998)
for more information visit www.zerosei.comune.re.it or www.domusacacdemy.com

Children's spaces
edited by Mark Dudek (Architectural Press 2005), ISBN 07506 5426 0
available from most bookstores

Design and construction of sustainable schools Volumes One and Two: Lessons from school buildings
in Norway and Germany (Gaia Architects and The Lighthouse, 2005),
Vol 1: ISBN 1 905061 072, Vol 2: ISBN 1 905061 080
to order hard copy email: schoolstate@scotland.gsi.gov.uk

Designing schools for the future: a practical guide
Rebecca Hodgson and Graham Leicester (Children in Scotland 2003), ISBN 1 901589 226
to order: www.childreninscotland.org.uk/pubdesign

Designs on my learning: a guide to involving young people in school design
(The Lighthouse 2005) ISBN 1 905061 064
to order: chrisopher.kane@thelighthouse.co.uk
to download pdf: www.thelighthouse.co.uk/page.php?page=projects&sub=pr-flat

Discovering architecture: civic education in architecture in Finland: Report
(The Finnish Association of Architects and the Arts Council of Finland 2001), ISBN 951 9307 10 9
for more information visit www.safa.fi or www.taiteenkeskustoimikunta.fi

Kindergarten architecture: space for the imagination (2nd edition)
Mark Dudek, (Spon Press, London 2000) ISBN 0 419 24520 0
available from most bookstores